I0823124

INTO THE UNKNOWN

THE MYSTERY OF UFOS

Kevin Cunningham

Mitchell Lane
PUBLISHERS

Mitchell Lane
PUBLISHERS

mitchelllanepub.com

2001 SW 31st Avenue
Hallandale, FL 33009

First Edition, 2026.
Author: Kevin Cunningham
Designer: Ed Morgan
Editor: Morgan Brody

Series: Into the Unknown
Title: The Mystery of UFOs

Library bound ISBN: 979-8-89260-738-4
eBook ISBN: 979-8-89260-741-4

Photo credits: cover p. 2, 3, 4, 5, 9, 15, 21, 25 freepik.com; p. 7 Alamy; p. 11, 17 wikimedia; p. 13, 19, 23, 27 Shutterstock

CONTENTS

CHAPTER ONE

FLYING SAUCERS

Kenneth A. Arnold went up in his small plane on June 24, 1947. He flew past Mount Ranier in Washington state. A bright flash startled him. He looked around. Nine round objects buzzed through the sky. The disks flew at high speed.

"I judged their size to be at least 100 feet wide," Arnold said. "I thought it was a new type of missile."

A newspaper interviewed Arnold. The reporters wrote the term "saucer-shaped objects" in their story.

CHAPTER ONE

The news went coast to coast. Reports used the term *flying saucer*. The attention embarrassed Arnold. But it was too late. Hundreds of reports of flying objects poured in. The most famous incident happened a few weeks after Arnold's report.

W. W. "Mac" Brazel worked on a New Mexico ranch. He found scattered **debris**. The debris included foil, tape, and bits of rubber. Military investigators took the material to their base in Roswell, New Mexico.

An Air Force report claimed Brazel had found a flying disc. But the story changed the next day. The debris came from a balloon, a Roswell paper said. In 1972, the Air Force admitted the balloon was part of a secret military project.

In the meantime, the Air Force investigated flying saucers. Captain Edward J. Ruppelt worked on the project. He renamed the aircraft *unidentified flying objects*, or UFOs.

FAST FACT

Some World War II pilots saw lights following their planes. American airmen nicknamed the lights *foo fighters*. A group of scientists could not explain foo fighters.

CHAPTER TWO

UP IN THE SKY

The United States and a country called the Soviet Union fought together in World War II. The Soviet Union was made up of Russia and 14 nearby nations. The US and the Soviet Union became enemies soon after the war ended.

The two countries began the **Cold War**. Each side feared an attack. The American military worked on new aircraft, ships, and weapons. The Soviets did the same.

CHAPTER TWO

The first UFO sightings happened early in the Cold War. The military needed to find answers. The objects might be secret Soviet aircraft. UFOs also caused fear across the country. The Air Force hoped to calm down the public.

The Air Force assigned officers to check out the stories. Project Blue Book started in 1952. Investigators kept files on every sighting.

Project Blue Book and two other projects looked at 12,618 UFO reports. Investigators called most sightings airplanes, balloons, satellites, or even swamp gas. The Air Force failed to explain 701 cases.

FAST FACT

A kind of cloud called lenticular clouds sometimes look like a flying saucer. Lenticular clouds form most often next to mountaintops. Air flowing over the mountain meets moisture on the other side. The clouds often form into saucer or pancake shapes.

CHAPTER TWO

New reports came in every year. But the public had accepted the Cold War. Fear died down.

UFO stories turned into **folklore**. Famous sightings became part of local history. Towns in New Hampshire and Mississippi put up markers with stories of sightings. People went to conventions to hear stories. Roswell, New Mexico, celebrated UFOs at a summer festival. Comics, TV shows, movies, and books borrowed details from UFO folklore.

FAST FACT

Every July 2, believers (and anyone else) celebrate World UFO Day. The famous crash at Roswell, New Mexico, happened on July 2. Some people observe a second World UFO Day on June 24. That's the day of the year Kenneth A. Arnold spotted flying saucers.

CHAPTER THREE

SIGHTINGS AND STORIES

The UFO puzzle remained unsolved. Sightings continued. Not everyone trusted the Air Force explanations. Believers wanted to show alien spacecraft existed. Some of them invented **conspiracy theories**. The theories often accused the government of holding back information.

Some UFO stories, believers said, offered scientific evidence.

CHAPTER THREE

Kansas teen Ron Johnson lived near Delphos, Kansas. One night in 1971 he walked his dog. A flying object floated about 75 feet ahead. Its bright lights almost blinded him. Johnson brought out his parents. The family watched the object fly away. It left a glowing ring on the ground. Ron's mother touched the ring. Her fingers went numb.

Betty Cash and Vickie Landrum drove down a Texas highway. Seven-year-old Colby Landrum sat in the back seat. A diamond-shaped object blocked the road. It was "maybe as large, if not larger than, a water tower," Cash said. Flames shot out of the craft.

FAST FACT

Four lights appeared over Scottsdale, Arizona, in 1997. A teen took a video. Hundreds of people saw the UFOs. The lights moved slowly. They flew in a V shape. At times they blinked. Some people said the lights appeared to be on a large object.

CHAPTER THREE

The adults moved closer. Intense heat drove them back. The door handle burned Cash's hand. The dashboard inside the car melted.

Cash and Landrum claimed the UFO's heat damaged the pavement. They also said military helicopters chased away the object. Cash became sick later that night. She went to the hospital.

Believers had always investigated sightings. They kept doing so. But **skeptics** started to dig into cases. They used a just-the-facts approach. Proof of UFOs as spaceships fell apart. And then the military told its own secrets.

FAST FACT

Area 51 is a big part of UFO folklore. The Nevada military base tests secret military equipment. Many UFO supporters believe in a conspiracy theory. They think the government stores spacecraft and even alien bodies at Area 51.

CHAPTER FOUR

IS THE TRUTH OUT THERE?

Skeptics look at UFOs with the **scientific method**. The method tests an idea. It involves making a prediction. Then investigators gather **data**. The data may support the prediction. It may not.

Scientists and others look at UFO cases using evidence as data.

Donald R. Prothero and Timothy D. Callahan studied the Ron Johnson sighting. A laboratory did scientific tests. The lab studied soil from the glowing ring.

A **bacterium** found in the soil lives around a kind of fungus. The fungus glows at night. It produces a white substance. The substance can cause numbness. The lab tests found the substance. That evidence could explain why Mrs. Johnson's fingers went numb.

CHAPTER FOUR

The research did not deny the Johnsons' UFO story. Fungi just seemed a *more likely* explanation than a visitor from space.

Betty Cash and the Landrums' story had problems, too. No one photographed the melted dashboard. The pavement was undamaged. The military disagreed that its helicopters flew in the area. Cash refused to show her medical records. Only the records could connect her illness to the UFO.

The Cold War ended in 1991. The US government slowly opened some of its secret files.

It turned out that tests on secret jet projects had led to UFO sightings. Area 51, a UFO hotspot, tested many secret aircraft. A 2024 report added that the military found no evidence of alien life.

FAST FACT

Bad air spreads diseases. The Earth is expanding. Canals crisscross Mars' surface. All of these beliefs once had support from many or most scientists. But science no longer takes these beliefs seriously. New evidence failed to support each idea.

CHAPTER FIVE

UFO HOAXES

Every so often, a person or group makes up a UFO sighting. The **hoax** gets attention. An image blows up on social media.

A hoax may find believers. The stories find their way into UFO folklore.

But almost all hoaxes quickly disappear. The hoaxer admits they faked the sighting. Or there's no evidence.

"The great saucer invasion" read the headline. It was 1967. UFO reports had spiked in the United Kingdom.

One morning people found six metal saucers across the southern UK. The military and police rushed into action. The silver objects could be carried by two people. Police drilled into one. It blew up. A slime made of flour and water covered the officers.

CHAPTER FIVE

Two young engineers admitted to the prank that day. They had built the objects with friends. No one imagined the fakes would cause a **panic**.

Today, the internet spreads hoaxes. A 2007 video showed UFOs buzzing over Haiti. Millions of people watched the video. It looked like evidence. A news site investigated. A computer animator admitted making the video. He created special effects for movies. His hoax video was a test. He wanted to see how people reacted.

Skeptics explain sightings. UFO believers prefer their own stories. News sites and podcasts still treat many UFO cases as unsolved mysteries. Fans repeat the details. Sharing draws people together. Folklore often creates these kinds of relationships.

But the science is clear. We have yet to see evidence that UFOs come from space.

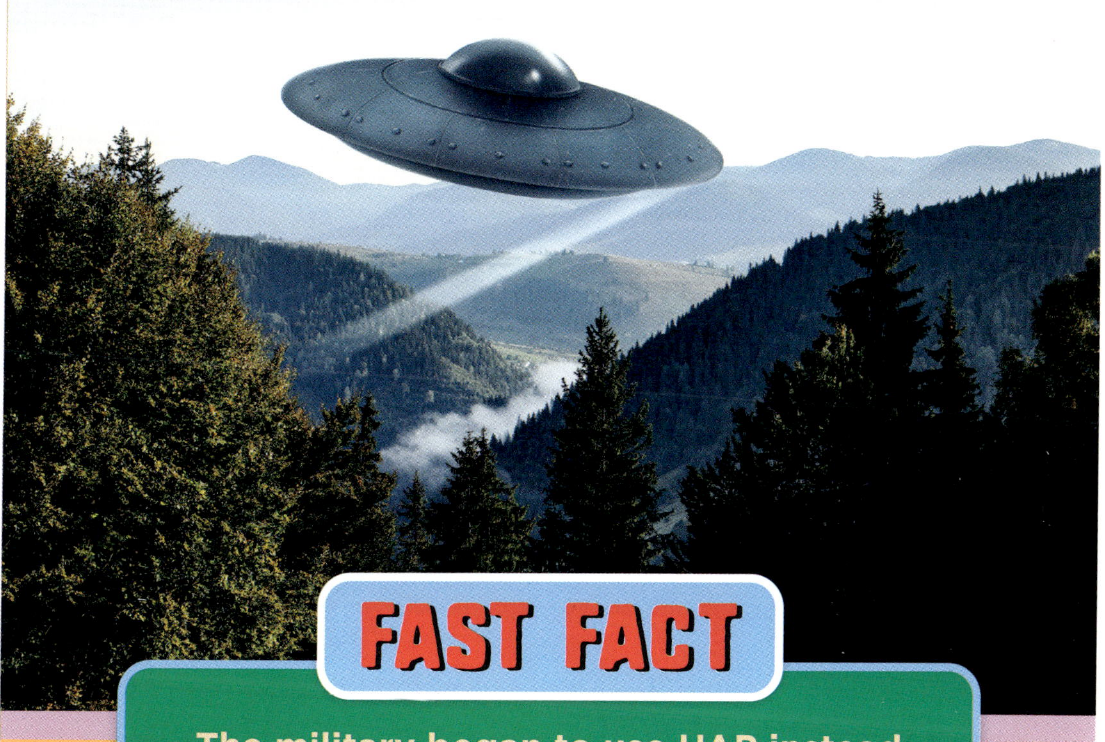

FAST FACT

The military began to use UAP instead of UFO in 2020. To many people, UFO meant conspiracy theories and ridiculous stories. Pilots and others often refused to report UFOs. They feared it would damage how others thought about them. UAP stands for *unidentified anomalous phenomena*.

TIMELINE

1945 The Cold War begins

1947 Kenneth A. Arnold reports "flying disks" near Mount Rainier

1947 W. W. "Mac" Brazel finds wreckage of an unknown aircraft near Roswell, New Mexico

1952 Project Blue Book begins to investigate UFO sightings

1967 A saucer invasion in the United Kingdom turns out to be a hoax

1971 Ron Johnson sees a UFO near Delphos, Kansas

2013 The US government admits Area 51 exists

2024 The US military says it has found no evidence of alien ships

GLOSSARY

bacterium (BAK-teer-ee-um)
A one-celled form of life that cannot be seen without a microscope

Cold War (KOLD WAR)
A period from 1945 to 1991 when the United States and Soviet Union opposed each other

conspiracy theory (ken-SPIR-e-see THE-o-ree)
A belief that powerful forces control or hide information about an event

data (DEY-da)
Evidence collected for analysis

debris (de-BREE)
Pieces of waste or remains

folklore (FOK-lor)
The beliefs and stories of a group or community of people

hoax (HOKS)
A fake or trick used to deceive others

panic (PA-nik)
Sudden fear or anxiety

scientific method (SI-en-TIF-ik ME-THed)
A list of tasks for testing scientific ideas

skeptics (SKEP-tiks)
People who doubt or questions an idea

FACT CHECK

1. **Sightings of UFOs began at the same time as which historical event?**

   A. The COVID-19 pandemic
   B. The Great Depression
   C. The Cold War
   D. The first moon landing

2. **Which part of the US military investigated UFO sightings?**

   A. The Coast Guard
   B. The Air Force
   C. The Navy
   D. The Space Force

3. **The flying saucer crash in Roswell, New Mexico, was really a crash of what object?**

   A. A balloon
   B. A top secret jet
   C. A blimp
   D. A drone

4. **Which one of the answers below is not part of the scientific method?**

   A. Gathering data
   B. Making a prediction
   C. Seeing if the data does or does not support the prediction
   D. Only using evidence that supports your prediction

Answers: C, B, A, D

FIND OUT MORE

IN PRINT

Kim, Carol. *Area 51 and UFO Mysteries*. North Mankato, MN: Capstone, 2022

Mason, Jenny. *UFOs*. New York: Children's Press, 2022.

Olson, Gillia M. *Curious about UFOs*. Mankato, MN: Amicus Publishing, 2022.

ON THE INTERNET

Encyclopedia Brittanica. "Is there proof of alien life?" Britannica.com. Undated. Video. www.britannica.com/video/what-the-fact-aliens-in-history/-258436

Encyclopedia Brittanica. "What Is the Scientific Method?" Brittanica.com. Undated. Video. www.britannica.com/video/did-you-know-scientific-method/-259089

Smithsonian Magazine. "The Mysterious Roswell Incident of 1947." Smithsonianmag.com via Youtube.com. Posted January 9, 2012. Video. www.youtube.com/watch?v=odUSnDgU-oo

INDEX

About the Author

Kevin Cunningham has written over 120 books on history, medicine, careers, and climate change. He lives near Chicago, Illinois. The UFO film *Close Encounters of the Third Kind* is one of his favorite movies and he always wanted to write a book about unidentified flying objects.